CHARLIE PUTH

SINGER & SONGWRITER

KATIE LAJINESS

Big Buddy Books
An Imprint of Abdo Publishing
abdobooks.com

BIG BUDDY POP BIOGRAPHIES

abdobooks.com

Published by Abdo Publishing, a division of ABDO, PO Box 398166, Minneapolis, Minnesota 55439.
Copyright © 2019 by Abdo Consulting Group, Inc. International copyrights reserved in all countries.
No part of this book may be reproduced in any form without written permission from the publisher.
Big Buddy Books™ is a trademark and logo of Abdo Publishing.

Printed in the United States of America, North Mankato, Minnesota.
102018
012019

THIS BOOK CONTAINS
RECYCLED MATERIALS

Cover Photo: Timothy Hiatt/Getty Images.
Interior Photos: Christopher Polk/Getty Images (p. 5); Dia Dipasupil/Getty Images (pp. 9, 23); Gustavo
    Caballero/Getty Images (p. 25); Jason Kempin/Getty Images (p. 11); Jemal Countess/Getty
    Images (pp. 13, 19); Kevin Winter/Getty Images (pp. 17, 21); Kevork Djansezian/Getty Images
    (p. 27); Michael Kovac/Getty Images (p. 15); Vivien Killilea/Getty Images (p. 29).

Coordinating Series Editor: Tamara L. Britton
Contributing Series Editor: Jill M. Roesler
Graphic Design: Jenny Christensen, Cody Laberda

Library of Congress Control Number: 2018948444

Publisher's Cataloging-in-Publication Data

Names: Lajiness, Katie, author.
Title: Charlie Puth / by Katie Lajiness.
Description: Minneapolis, Minnesota : Abdo Publishing, 2019 | Series: Big buddy
    pop biographies set 4 | Includes online resources and index.
Identifiers: ISBN 9781532118029 (lib. bdg.) | ISBN 9781532171062 (ebook)
Subjects: LCSH: Puth, Charlie, 1991- --Juvenile literature. | Singers--Biography--
    Juvenile literature. | Popular music--Juvenile literature. | Internet videos--
    Juvenile literature.
Classification: DDC 782.42164092 [B]--dc23

CONTENTS

POP STAR

Charlie Puth is a popular singer and songwriter. Many know him for his **pop** music. He has sung **duets** with other famous singers.

As a superstar, Charlie often appears on TV shows. He is also **interviewed** for magazines.

Charlie has won many **awards** for his hit albums and songs. Fans around the world love to see him **perform**!

SNAPSHOT

NAME:
Charles Otto Puth Jr.

BIRTHDAY:
December 2, 1991

BIRTHPLACE:
Rumson, New Jersey

POPULAR ALBUMS:
Nine Track Mind, Voicenotes

FAMILY TIES

Charles Otto Puth Jr. was born in Rumson, New Jersey, on December 2, 1991. His parents are Charles and Debra Puth. He has younger twin **siblings**, Stephen and Mikaela.

DID YOU KNOW?
Charlie's mom Debra is a music teacher.

WHERE IN THE WORLD?

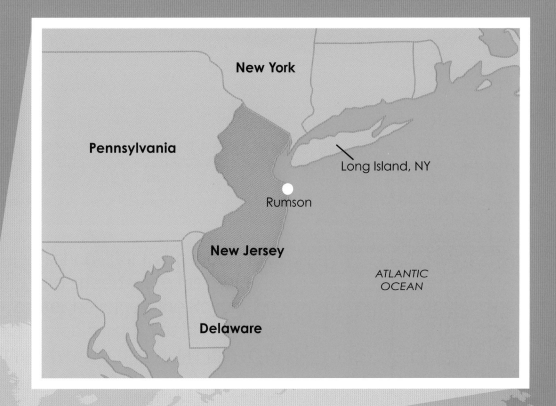

New York

Pennsylvania

Long Island, NY

Rumson

New Jersey

ATLANTIC
OCEAN

Delaware

EARLY YEARS

Early on, Charlie's mom knew her son had a great singing voice. He had **perfect pitch**. He began playing the piano when he was four years old. Later, he grew to love **jazz** music. So he began studying jazz piano at the Manhattan School of Music.

DID YOU KNOW?
Charlie attended the Berklee College of Music in Boston, Massachusetts.

Charlie has a scar on his right eyebrow. The scar is from where a dog bit him when he was a child.

STARTING OUT

While in college, Charlie and his friend Emily Luther sang a **duet**. Then he posted it on **social media**. This video helped the two win an online contest called "Can You Sing?"

TV host Ellen DeGeneres liked Charlie's video. She asked Charlie and Emily to sing on her show. Ellen signed the two to her new music label. Sadly, the album did not work out.

Charlie and Emily sang Adele's "Someone Like You" on YouTube.

Charlie did not give up on his dreams of being a **pop** star. He continued to make music and even **released** his own **EP** online. After years of hard work, Charlie finally joined Atlantic Records in 2015!

In 2015, Charlie appeared on *Good Morning America* with Joe Jonas *(center)* and host Ginger Zee *(left)*.

BIG VOICE

After signing with Atlantic Records, Charlie moved to Los Angeles, California. Two days after the move, he wrote "See You Again" for the movie *Furious 7*. It reached number one on the *Billboard* Hot 100 music chart.

In 2018, Charlie sang "If You Leave Me Now" with the music group Boyz II Men. He sang the song **a cappella**.

Rapper Wiz Khalifa *(right)* worked with Charlie on the song "See You Again" in 2015. Billions of people have watched the video on YouTube.

In 2016, singer Selena Gomez joined Charlie in the song "We Don't Talk Anymore." They sang onstage together during the last show of her US tour. This was the first time they **performed** together live.

The talented singer has co-written songs for Maroon 5, Pitbull, and Jason Derulo.

FAN FAVORITE

Charlie built his **career** on **social media**. First, he used YouTube to share videos. As he gained more fans, he also communicated on Facebook, Twitter, and Instagram. This helped him keep in contact with his fans every day.

Charlie has millions of Twitter followers. Many fans press the "like" button to show support.

Charlie often tours the country to **perform** his latest music. In 2015, he went on tour with singer Meghan Trainor. They sang their **duet** called "Marvin Gaye."

In March and April 2016, Charlie played 20 shows to **promote** his *Nine Track Mind* album. The next year, he joined superstar Shawn Mendes on a world tour.

In 2015, Charlie wrote the song "Marvin Gaye." He and pop star Meghan Trainor *(right)* performed it at the 2015 American Music Awards.

GIFTED SONGWRITER

Charlie is a talented songwriter. He writes the **lyrics** and records himself playing music in his home **studio**.

He wrote the hit songs "Attention" and "How Long." And he has helped other artists write their songs.

DID YOU KNOW?
Charlie worked with Liam Payne after he left One Direction.

Not only does Charlie sing and write songs, he produces them, too. That means that he edits the song to create the final product.

AWARDS

Every year, the best singers and songwriters are **nominated** for music **awards**. Charlie was nominated for three **Grammy Awards** for the song "See You Again." And he has won two Teen Choice Awards and two *Billboard* Music Awards.

In 2017, Charlie appeared as himself in the CBS TV show *Life in Pieces*.

GIVING BACK

Charlie uses his voice to raise money for good causes. He sang "Attention" and "One Call Away" to kids at a hospital in Atlanta, Georgia.

In 2018, Charlie was a special guest at an education event. He **performed** in front of 1,400 guests. The event raised more than $2 million to help schools in Los Angeles.

In 2016, Charlie attended the Stand Up To Cancer event in Los Angeles. This group raises money to help fight a condition called cancer.

BUZZ

In 2018, Charlie **released** his second full album called *Voicenotes*. It is a mix of **jazz**, **R&B**, and **pop** music.

Charlie is a very successful singer and songwriter. Fans are excited to see what he does next!

DID YOU KNOW ?

Charlie released the single "Done For Me" with singer Kehlani. The song has millions of YouTube views.

Charlie went on tour with singer Hailee Steinfeld *(right)* in 2018. The two performed in 32 cities across North America.

GLOSSARY

a cappella without accompanying instrumental music.

award something that is given in recognition of good work or a good act.

career work a person does to earn money for a living.

duet a song performed by two people.

EP extended play. A music recording with more than one song, but fewer than a full album.

Grammy Award any of the awards given each year by the National Academy of Recording Arts and Sciences. Grammy Awards honor the year's best accomplishments in music.

interview to ask someone a series of questions.

jazz a form of American music that features lively and unusual beats. It first became popular in the early 1900s.

lyrics the words to a song.

nominate to name as a possible winner.

perfect pitch the ability to recognize the pitch of a note or to produce any given note.

perform to do something in front of an audience.

pop relating to popular music.

promote to help something become known.

R&B a form of popular music that features a strong beat. It is inspired by jazz, gospel, and blues styles.

release to make available to the public.

sibling a brother or a sister.

social media a form of communication on the Internet where people can share information, messages, and videos. It may include blogs and online groups.

studio a place where music is recorded.

ONLINE RESOURCES

Booklinks
NONFICTION NETWORK
FREE! ONLINE NONFICTION RESOURCES

To learn more about Charlie Puth, visit **abdobookslinks.com**. These links are routinely monitored and updated to provide the most current information available.

INDEX